THE LITTLE BOOK OF
DAD

Published by OH!
20 Mortimer Street
London W1T 3JW

Text © 2021 OH!
Design © 2021 OH!

ISBN 978-1-80069-016-5

Compiled by: Malcolm Croft
Editorial: Theresa Bebbington
Project manager: Russell Porter
Design: Tony Seddon
Production: Freencky Portas

A CIP catalogue record for this book is available from the British Library

Printed in Dubai

10 9 8 7 6 5 4 3 2 1

Illustrations: Freepik.com

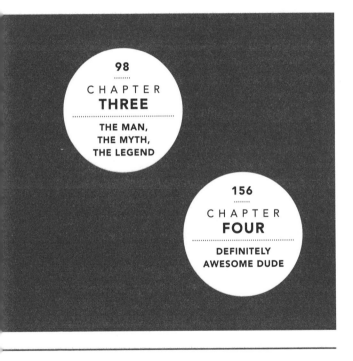

98

CHAPTER
THREE

THE MAN,
THE MYTH,
THE LEGEND

156

CHAPTER
FOUR

DEFINITELY
AWESOME DUDE

INTRODUCTION

Their bellies may stretch their spandex beyond saving and their capes may only fly on very windy days, but – make no mistake – dads are *real* superheroes. So, jog on, Iron Man.

Yes, despite being underpaid, under-appreciated, overworked and unable to remember the last time they were allowed a day off, being a dad is the world's greatest job. From taxi-ing teenagers to juggling chores, picking up stuff from the floor to constantly being kneed in the nuts, dads may make parenting look like a lot of fun but, as any dad will admit, being a father is no walk in the park. Even if there is also a lot of that too.

This *Little Book of Dad* is a celebration of dadhood, daddy-ing and all the dad-based shenanigans that comes with raising children to an acceptable standard. And this tiny tome couldn't be more timely.

THE LITTLE BOOK OF
DAD

PERFECT WORDS
FOR AWESOME DADS

CONTENTS

INTRODUCTION - 6

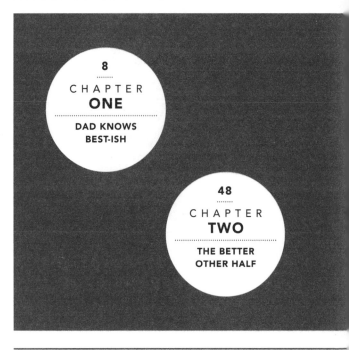

8

CHAPTER
ONE

DAD KNOWS
BEST-ISH

48

CHAPTER
TWO

THE BETTER
OTHER HALF

With Netflix, YouTube, Fortnite and *Peppa Pig* doing much of the heavy lifting these days, there has never been a better time in history to just sit back, relax and enjoy the wonders of what the hell happened to your life and getting some much needed perspective.

We all know dads are pretty important, but they're rarely celebrated. This little daddy-pedia is all about putting that to rights. Inside you'll find a wealth of fabulous facts, stats, wit and quips, not to mention a healthy dose of paternal wisdom. It's a book that will make you chuckle out loud and remind you of what really matters. As comedian Mike Myers had it, "Anyone who tells you fatherhood is the greatest thing that can happen to you, they are understating it."

Dads simply are the best, and we love them.

Enjoy!

CHAPTER
ONE

THE LITTLE BOOK OF

DAD

PERFECT WORDS
FOR AWESOME DADS

CONTENTS

INTRODUCTION - 6

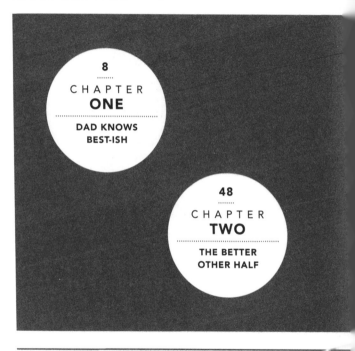

8

CHAPTER
ONE

**DAD KNOWS
BEST-ISH**

48

CHAPTER
TWO

**THE BETTER
OTHER HALF**

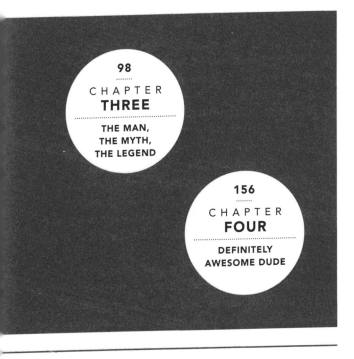

98

CHAPTER
THREE

THE MAN,
THE MYTH,
THE LEGEND

156

CHAPTER
FOUR

DEFINITELY
AWESOME DUDE

INTRODUCTION

Their bellies may stretch their spandex beyond saving and their capes may only fly on very windy days, but – make no mistake – dads are *real* superheroes. So, jog on, Iron Man.

Yes, despite being underpaid, under-appreciated, overworked and unable to remember the last time they were allowed a day off, being a dad is the world's greatest job. From taxi-ing teenagers to juggling chores, picking up stuff from the floor to constantly being kneed in the nuts, dads may make parenting look like a lot of fun but, as any dad will admit, being a father is no walk in the park. Even if there is also a lot of that too.

This *Little Book of Dad* is a celebration of dad-hood, daddy-ing and all the dad-based shenanigans that comes with raising children to an acceptable standard. And this tiny tome couldn't be more timely.

With Netflix, YouTube, Fortnite and *Peppa Pig* doing much of the heavy lifting these days, there has never been a better time in history to just sit back, relax and enjoy the wonders of what the hell happened to your life and getting some much needed perspective.

We all know dads are pretty important, but they're rarely celebrated. This little daddy-pedia is all about putting that to rights. Inside you'll find a wealth of fabulous facts, stats, wit and quips, not to mention a healthy dose of paternal wisdom. It's a book that will make you chuckle out loud and remind you of what really matters. As comedian Mike Myers had it, "Anyone who tells you fatherhood is the greatest thing that can happen to you, they are understating it."

Dads simply are the best, and we love them.

Enjoy!

CHAPTER
ONE

Dad Knows Best-ish

Say what you want about dads
- and the kids will - but when
it comes to knowing how to get
things done, dads know just the
right person to call: their dad.
Because dads know best.

Doodah / *duːda* / (UK) or doodad / *duːdad* (U.S.)

noun

a gadget or object whose name the speaker does not know or cannot recall.

"Has anyone seen the, er, *doodah* that turns the TV on?"*

Named after forgetful dads, no doubt.

In the 1970s, only six U.S. men identified themselves as stay-at-home parents. Not

6 per cent – *six men*,

in the entire country.*

Source: *Huffington Post*

Today, 2.4 million U.S. dads stay-at-home.

Types of Dad #1:
The Hider

This type of dad is a rare sight. If he's not in the garage "tinkering" or in the loft "sorting" or in his man cave "working", the Hider tries his hardest to be somewhere everyone else in his family is not. So, are you the Hider?

Dad Joke #1

Why couldn't the bicycle stand up by itself?

It was too tired.

Dad-isms #1

1. Fight among yourselves.

2. You're going out looking like that?

3. When I was a boy/in my day…

4. There's nothing a little
duct tape can't fix

5. As long as you live under my roof.
My house, my rules…

6. I paid good money for that.

7. Don't spend it all at once.

8. They don't make them like they used to.

9. What's the damage?

10. That's how they get you.

Father's Day Playlist #1:
Classics

1. *My Father's Eyes*, Eric Clapton

2. *Father and Daughter*, Paul Simon

3. *Father to Son*, Queen

4. *Papa Don't Preach*, Madonna

5. *Papa's Got a Brand New Bag*, James Brown

6. *My Father's House*, Bruce Springsteen

7. *Cat's in the Cradle*, Harry Chapin

8. *Father and Son*, Yusuf Islam /
Cat Stevens

9. *Daddy Lessons*, Beyoncé featuring
Dixie Chicks

10. *Papa Was a Rolling Stone*,
The Temptations

Smile because you're a father. *Laugh* because there is nothing you can do about it. *Cry* because you're exhausted.

Dad's Mantra

Ask your mother.

Parenting Paradox #1

The only thing better than being a dad is sleeping in late.

New dads achieve
4 hours and 44 minutes
of sleep a night during
the first year of their baby's
life. Over the same time,
dads sleep **59 per cent** less
than the recommended
8 hours a night, losing the
equivalent of

50 nights of sleep!

Source: *Independent*

You Know You're a Dad #1 When...

You hide in the bathroom.

(Anything for a moment of peace and quiet.)

Lies Dads Tell #1

1. I can see it from here!

2. Go hide, I'll come find you!

3. I don't make the rules!

4. I'm just going to lay down and rest my eyes for a second.

5. I'm not going to say it again!

6. When you're an adult you can do what you want.

KEEP
CALM
AND
CARRY
AN iPAD

Dad Joke #2

Dad, did you get a haircut?

No, I got them all cut!

** 66**

My father worked for the same firm for 12 years. They fired him and replaced him with a tiny gadget that does everything my father does, only much better. The depressing thing is my mother ran out and bought one.

99

Woody Allen

Shakespeare Does Dads #1

Why, 'tis a happy
thing / To be
the father unto
many sons.

Henry VI, Part 3, Act 3, Scene 2

"

My Father had a profound influence on me.
He was a lunatic.

"

Spike Milligan

Why don't eggs tell jokes?

They'd crack each other up.

Perfect Father's Day Movie: *Back to the Future*

The 1985 sci-fi blockbuster is perfect for Father's Day. The film sees Marty McFly (Michael J. Fox) accidently travel back in time to 1955. In that timeline, Marty must befriend his own high-school student dad to ensure he falls in love with his own teenage mum – and not Marty himself!

"

Wait a minute, Doc, are you trying to tell me that my mother has got the hots for me?

"

Marty McFly, *Back to the Future*, 1985

In 1982, **_43 per cent_** of dads had never changed a diaper or nappy. By 2000, this had declined to just

3 per cent.

Source: _The Telegraph_

Russian peasant Feodor Vassilyev (1707-1782) owns the record for fathering the most children, born to just one poor woman.

69 children!

Among this throng there were four sets of quadruplets, seven sets of triplets, and 16 pairs of twins.

Source: BBC

27
per cent

of children think
of their father as their
playtime favourite, with
their mother second at

24 per cent

Don't tell Mum!

Source: *The Guardian*

Dad Facts #1

The first founding father of the USA, George Washington, had no children of his own. It is believed that Washington contracted a type of tuberculosis in childhood that left him sterile.

Proud Dad: Harry Truman

The thirty-third president of the USA, Harry Truman, was a proud father. In 1950, after a *Washington Post* music critic gave Truman's daughter Margaret's concert a negative review, Truman responded in an unpresidential manner: "Someday I hope to meet you. When that happens you'll need a new nose, a lot of beefsteak for black eyes, and perhaps a supporter below!"

66

I'm a cool dad, that's my thang. I'm hip, I surf the web, I text. LOL: laugh out loud, OMG: Oh my god, WTF: Why the face...

99

Phil Dunphy, *Modern Family*

Dad Joke #4

I don't trust stairs. They're always up to something.

66

The heart of
a father is the
masterpiece
of nature.

99

Prevost Abbe

"

Whenever one of my children says, 'Goodnight, daddy,' I always think to myself, 'you don't mean that.'

Jim Gaffigan

"

Father! To God
Himself we cannot
give a holier name.

"

William Wordsworth, *Ecclesiastical Sonnets*, 1821–22

66

A man who doesn't spend time with his family can never be a real man.

99

The Godfather, 1972,
directed by Francis Ford Coppola

> Your father, Jo. He never loses patience, never doubts or complains, but always hopes, and works and waits so cheerfully that one is ashamed to do otherwise before him.

Little Women, Louisa May Alcott, 1868

Marriage is like a coffin and each kid is another nail.

Homer Simpson,
The Simpsons, Season 14, Episode 2

In 2019, the UK's Child Poverty Action Group published a definitive report that declared: raising a child to the age of *18* costs a two-parent family

£151,000 ($200,000).

Source: Child Poverty Action Group

Dad, Da-da, Daddy-O #1

Across the world, there are many words used to describe daddies...

1. Afrikaans - *Pappa*

2. Filipino - *Taytay*

3. Welsh - *Tad*

4. Turkish - *Baba*

5. Spanish - *Papá*

6. Swahili - *Mzazi*

7. Swedish - *Pappa*

8. Slovak - *Otec*

9. Polish - *Tata*

10. Portuguese - *Pai*

Dad Icon: Darth Vader

"

No... *I* am your father.

"

**Darth Vader, *The Empire Strikes Back*, 1980,
directed by Irvin Kershner**

Daddy Drink:
Long Island Iced Tea

The booziest cocktail known to man, the Long Island Iced Tea will ensure all dads are deemed unfit for purpose and snoozing by 1 pm. So, perfect for Father's Day.

Serving Suggestion:
Ice
25ml/1 oz gin
25ml/1 oz tequila
25ml/1 oz white rum
25ml/1 oz vodka
25ml/1 oz triple sec
25ml/1 oz simple syrup
50ml/2 oz freshly squeezed lime juice
Cola
Lime wedge

Make it Right:
Add ice to a tall glass, pour in the gin, tequila, rum, vodka, triple sec, simple syrup and lime juice, then top up with cola. Serve with a lime wedge – it counts as a serving of fruit. Stir. Sip. Snooze.

CHAPTER
TWO

The Better Other Half

Dads often play second fiddle to mums, but when mums absolutely need to get something important done – like undo the mustard jar or reach a high shelf – they never accept any substitutions: they yell for dad. He's always got just the right tool for the job.

Types of Dad #2:
The
Odd-Jobber

The Odd-Jobber is the type of dad who loves a job and is always on the lookout for something to do. He is always the first to offer a teenager a lift, clean the dishes or change a light bulb. This type of dad hates to be bored. Are you an Odd-Jobber?

Father's Day

Every dad looks forward to Father's Day! But did you know that the origins of Father's Day date back to 1909, when Sonora Dodd, from Spokane, Washington, USA, first put forward the proposal for a "Father's Day" to honour her remarkable father.

In 1972, America's President Richard Nixon made the day a national holiday - the only Western nation to do so.

A 2014 study revealed that dads who do household chores have more ambitious daughters - as well as daughters with more broad definitions of gender roles.

Source: University of British Columbia

Dad's the Word

The word "father" originates from the ye Olde English word "fæder"* (meaning "supreme being", naturally), but "dad" comes from "da da", the sound made by infants trying to make soft consonants. "Da da" is the most natural sound an infant can make (it requires no mouth muscle movement) and is often uttered before "ma ma".

Source: Fatherly

* The word originated from the Proto-Indo-European "pəter"*. A phonetic shift from "p" to "f" occurred during the Middle English period (1066-1500s).

66

With sons and fathers, there's an inexplicable connection and imprint that your father leaves on you.

99

Brad Pitt

66

My father didn't
tell me how to live;
he lived, and let me
watch him do it.

99

Clarence Budington Kelland

Daedalus, the creator of the labyrinth (you know, the huge maze located under the court of King Minos of Crete, where the Minotaur lived) is not the most famous father in Greek mythology. But he is, perhaps, the most caring. Daedalus told his first-born son, Icarus, not to fly too close to the sun or the wax in his wings would melt.

Naturally, Icarus didn't listen.

On February 11, 2020,
the world said goodbye to its oldest
father, Ramjit Raghav. He died
at the age of 104.
He became a parent at the age of

to his second son, named Ramjeet.

(His first son
was born when Ramjit was... 94.)

Source: Daily Mail.com

"

Anyone who tells you fatherhood is the greatest thing that can happen to you, they are understating it.

Mike Myers

To be the father of growing daughters is to understand... that your heart is running around inside someone else's body. It also makes me quite astonishingly calm at the thought of death: I know whom I would die to protect...

Christopher Hitchens

UK dads, on average, spend **_35 minutes_** playing with their children every weekday.
In 1974, it was registered as only

5 minutes a day.

Source: _The Guardian_

43 per cent of fathers agreed that their favourite years of parenting were when their children were in the **_6-12 years_** age group. Only 13 per cent thought the 13-17 years age group was the best.

Source: *Independent*

In 2019, in the USA, Hallmark sold ***113 million cards*** for Mother's Day and ***72 million*** for Father's Day – one for each father (*according to the U.S. Census Bureau*).

Source: Hallmark

Dad Bods

A dad bod is considered the perfect balance between regular exercise and downright laziness. A dad who is active but doesn't count calories, keeping their bodies at a relative median for their age and height. In a 2020 study, 65 per cent of women said they thought the dad bod was "sexy", a 10 per cent rise compared to 2018.

When it comes to a "dad bod", 78 per cent of partners agree that confidence is king.

Source: *Newsweek*

Today, only ***24 per cent*** of children are financially independent by 22 years old, compared with

32 per cent in 1980.

Kids need daddy's (wallet) more than ever before.

Source: Pew Research Centre

Dad Joke #5

What do you call someone with no body and no nose?

Nobody knows.

"

Don't worry that children never listen to you; worry that they are always watching you.

"

Robert Fulghum

66

When I was a boy of 14, my father was so ignorant, I could hardly stand to have the old man around. But when I got to be 21, I was astonished at how much the old man had learned in seven years.

99

Mark Twain

Dad Joke #6

Dad, can you put my shoes on?

No, I don't think they'll fit me..

66

By the time a man realizes that maybe his father was right, he usually has a son who thinks he's wrong.

Charles Wadsworth

❝

From the moment she's born a man's daughter is the centre of his universe. You give her love, you give her encouragement, you watch her grow into a strong confident woman. And then one day you come face to face with the love of her life...

❞

Ned Fleming, *Why Him?*

In 2020, millennials spent more on their fathers for Father's Day than any previous generation, with each purchase averaging £115 ($150).

Of each purchase, 41 per cent was bought on the condition that it was unique or different.

Source: National Retail Federation

The Guinness Book of World Records claims that Moulay Ismail (1672–1727), a Moroccan sultan, fathered the highest number of children:

1,703!

More than four wives and 500 other women helped him secure the world record.

One in 200 men

are direct descendants
of Genghis Khan.

Source: *Discover Magazine*

The earliest inscribed record of a Father's Day "card" is around 4,000 years old. It was found in the ruins of Babylon (modern-day Iraq). A young boy, Elmesu, carved the clay tablet with a stylus and wrote a message for his father that wished him good health and a long life.

Source: Hallmark

Children need fathers.
But dads *need* kids –
54 per cent of dads
feel better about themselves
because they're a dad.

Source: Pew Research Centre

"

Any man can be
a father, but it takes
someone special
to be a dad.

"

Anne Geddes

Shakespeare Does Dads #2

"

I would my father look'd
but with my eyes.

"

A Midsummer Night's Dream, Act 1, Scene 1

Teen girls without a father are seven times more likely to become pregnant as a teenager.

Source: U.S. Census Bureau

The average age to become a father in the UK is **33.6 years old**. A generation ago it was 24 years old. Today, in the USA, it is 31 years old.

Source: *Harper's Bazaar*

Father's Day Playlist #2: *For Dad*

1. *Daughters*, John Mayer

2. *Beautiful Boy*, John Lennon

3. *Song for Dad*, Keith Urban

4. *Dance with My Father*, Luther Vandross

5. *My Daddy Knows Best*, The Marvelettes

6. *Song for My Father*, Sarah McLachlan

7. *Boy Named Sue*, Johnny Cash

8. *Let Me Be the Man My Daddy Was*, The Chi-Lites

9. *The Greatest Man I Never Knew*, Reba McEntire

10. *Living Years*, Mike + the Mechanics

I've done all kinds of cool things as an actor: I've jumped out of helicopters and done some daring stunts and played baseball in a professional stadium, but none of it means anything compared to being somebody's daddy.

Chris Pratt

Classic Films for Father's Day

1. *Father's Day* (1997)

2. *Mr. Mom* (1983)

3. *Parenthood* (1989)

4. *National Lampoon's Vacation* (1983)

5. *Father of the Bride* (1991)

6. *Indiana Jones and the Last Crusade* (1989)

7. *The Parent Trap* (1998)

8. *Mrs. Doubtfire* (1993)

9. *Cheaper By the Dozen* (2003)

10. *Three Men and a Baby* (1987)

Iconic evolutionary
biologist Charles Darwin
was a huge fan of passing
on his DNA, if not
necessarily always for
scientific purposes.
He was a doting dad to
10 children.

Things Only New Fathers Do...

1. Wet the baby's head down the pub or in a bar
(with beer or whisky).

2. Buy a parenting manual (they'll never read).

3. Google "How to be a dad".

4. Buy baby gadgets (they'll never use).

5. Take photos of their babies first poos (stools).

6. Watch their baby sleep (despite their
own extreme exhaustion).

7. Triple check the infant car seat
(and tidy the car).

8. Find themselves wondering around
a supermarket in a daze.

9. Realize that nothing will ever be the same again.

10. Appreciate their own parents more
than they ever have.

66

I thought I would be more inspired to have all these new feelings to talk about, but I really just want to hang out with my daughter.

99

Jay-Z

Dad's Best Brands

1. Apple
2. Under Armour
3. Nike
4. Netflix
5. Amazon
6. Disney
7. Lego
8. Levi's
9. Kobalt Tools
10. Harley-Davison*

Source: Business Insider

* The top 10 brands for men without kids included: Bose, Microsoft, Harley-Davidson, Sony, Disney, Microsoft, Apple, Nike, Under Armour, and BMW.

Six Top Tips for New Dads

1. Look after yourself - shower, eat, sleep, exercise.

2. Enjoy one on one time with the baby - let mum sleep.

3. Make mum cups of tea and meals.

4. Accept help whenever someone offers.

5. Talk to your baby.

6. Change all the nappies you can get your hands on.

In 2020, dads are
less likely to share their
life, photos, experiences
and thoughts on social
media than they were
in 2019, a drop to

42 per cent

from 62.5 per cent.

Source: Vista Village

Be the dad that
everyone wishes
they had.

Fatherhood is...
like banging your
head against a very
cute and adorable
brick wall.

Perks of the Job

1. No one raises an eyebrow if you look dishevelled.

2. All leftovers are yours.

3. Little servants bring you things.

4. You get to say "I told you so" more often.

5. Being asleep by 9 pm.

DON'T PANIC!

*(Other dads don't know
what they're doing either.)*

Parenting Paradox #2

Even when you
feel your worst you'll
do your best.

Dads will pace the equivalent of 2 miles while rocking their baby each day and night, totting up to

730 miles

– the equivalent of 28 marathons! – over a 365-day period.

Source: *Independent*

> **"**
>
> My dad always said, 'Champ, the measure of a man is not how often he is knocked down, but how quickly he gets up.'
>
> **"**

U.S. President Joe Biden

"

I never used to get too
wound up or worried about
things. But now, as a father, the
smallest little things, you well up
a little more; you get affected by
the things that happen around
the world a lot more.

"

Prince William

Always teach your children to say "thank you" after wiping their bum. Let them know it was a service you provided, not a pleasure they should always just expect.

CHAPTER
THREE

The Man, the Myth, the Legend

Humans are possibly the only species on Earth where the man is both myth and legend – except Bigfoot, perhaps. Yes, it's true: dads are universally beloved for their awesomeness. It's just a shame they know it too!

Of new fathers,
8 per cent forget the
name of their baby in a
conversation.

*(Due to exhaustion, we
should add!)*

Source: *Independent*

Dad Joke #7

What do you call a donkey with only three legs?

A wonkey!

THE MAN, THE MYTH, THE LEGEND

You Know You're a Dad #2 When...

You set up a TV in the garage.

Dad-isms #2

1. You make a better door than a window.

2. Where was the last place you left it?

3. Don't make me turn this car around.

4. Money doesn't grow on trees.

5. Don't use that tone with me.

6. Do you think I'm made of money?

7. I'm not going to tell you again.

8. I'm not your chauffeur.

9. When you're as old as me, we can talk.

10. Turn those lights off.

There are

1.5 billion

fathers in the world.

Source: Huffington Post

Shakespeare Does Dads #3

> If by chance I talk a little wild, forgive me; I had it from my father.

Henry VIII, Act 1, Scene 4

Men release about 100 million sperm each time they make love. But only a few hundred reach a female's egg. And the egg has special receptors to ensure only one sperm gets in. So, your little miracle is a one-in-a-100-*million* shot!

Source: *Independent*

On average,
a new dad puts on
4.4 extra pounds
in his child's first year.

Source: *Daily Mail*

Daughters spend
50 per cent more on
Father's Day gifts
for their dad than their
brotherly counterparts.

Source: Much Needed

Fathers in the USA tend to make 40 per cent more money than men without kids and are usually paid more after they have children. And fathers are more likely to be hired than childless men.

Source: *New York Times*

Dad Facts #2

The only father-daughter collaboration in music history to hit the No.1 spot was the 1967 hit single *Something Stupid* by Frank and Nancy Sinatra.

Every father should remember one day his son will follow his example, not his advice.

Charles Kettering

66

All that I have, all that I've learned,
everything I feel... all this, and more,
I... I bequeath you, my son. You will
carry me inside you, all the days of
your life. You will make my strength
your own, and see my life through
your eyes, as your life will be seen
through mine. The son becomes the
father, and the father the son. This
is all I... all I can send you, Kal-El.

99

Jor-El, *Superman*, 1978, directed by Richard Donner

You Know You're a Dad #3 When...

You can't remember the last time you saw a film all the way through.

"

The greatest tribute a boy can give to his father is to say, 'When I grow up, I want to be just like my dad.'

"

Billy Graham

Fathers with young daughters are more attentive and responsive to their daughters' needs than fathers with young sons.

Source: American Psychological Association

Old Wives' Tale

In the middle ages, women believed they had more chance of siring a son if they asked their husbands to turn their faces eastwards during sex.

66

I believe that what we become depends on what our fathers teach us at odd moments, when they aren't trying to teach us. We are formed by little scraps of wisdom.

99

Umberto Eco

Dad, Da-da, Daddy-O #2

1. Persian/Farsi - *Pedar*
2. Nepali - *Buwa*
3. Maori - *Haakoro*
4. Mandarin Chinese - *Ba*
5. Latvian - *Tevs*
6. Korean - *Appa*
7. Japanese - *Otosan*
8. Italian - *Babbo*
9. Hindi - *Pita-ji*
10. Hebrew - *Abba*
11. German - *Papi*
12. French - *Papa*

Matilda: "I'm nothing like my father."

Ms. Trunchbull: "You're the spitting image. The apple never rots far from the tree!"

Matilda, 1986, directed by Danny DeVito
Based on Roald Dahl's book, *Matilda*

Types of Dad #3:

The Grump

This type of dad is loveable in his own little way. He is forever grumping around the house moaning about something – be it a new stain on the sofa or the TV is too loud. This dad is happiest when he's miserable. Are you the Grump?

A study in 2019 showed that dads who are more present, active and positive in their child's life are responsible for a

43 per cent

lift in their child's grades at school.

Source: Pew Research Centre

Vatertag, or Männertag (Men's Day), is Germany's very own twist on Father's Day.

Celebrated 40 days after Easter, Vatertag is a day off for dads and sons alike. Breakfast is consumed in bed and groups of men gather to drink beer that has been loaded onto wagons. They wheel the wagons through the local town all day long!

Source: Reader's Digest

You don't raise heroes, you raise sons. And if you treat them like sons, they'll turn out to be heroes, even if it's just in your own eyes.

Walter M. Schirra Sr

Lies Dads Tell #2

If you make silly faces while having your picture taken, it will stay like that.

Dad Joke #8

How many tickles does it take to make an octopus laugh?

Ten tickles.

A study by the University of North Carolina found that mammals are more like their fathers than their mothers in terms of genetic makeup. Even though we get the same amount of genetic mutations from our parents, we actually use

10 per cent more of the DNA

we get from fathers.

Source: *Independent*

Millennials, the largest generation of any in human history, are far more likely to buy meaningful "experiences" for their dads for Father's Day than gadgets, neckties and socks.

Source: National Retail Federation

The average 30-year-old dad passes on 55 mutations – changes in the DNA in a gene – to his child. Those mutations are what will make your child unique.

Source: Daily Mail

In 2020, due to the
COVID-19 pandemic,
45 per cent of people
were not able to see their
dads on Father's Day.

Source: Money.co.uk

Shakespeare Does Dads #4

66

My father's wit, and my mother's tongue, assist me!

99

Love's Labour's Lost, Act 1, Scene 2

66

You know how it is
with fathers, you
never escape the idea
that maybe after all
they're right.

99

John Updike

Dad-isms #3

1. Don't make me come back there.

2. One day, you'll thank me.

3. I brought you into this world, and I can take you out of it.

4. A little hard work never hurt anybody.

5. No one said life was fair.

6. Ask a stupid question, you'll get a stupid answer.

7. Act your age, not your shoe size.

8. I am not your personal taxi service.

9. You treat this house like a hotel!

10. It's like talking to a brick wall!

"

When I was a young man, I thought life was all about me. But then my daughters came into my world with all their curiosity and mischief and those smiles that never fail to fill my heart and light up my day. And suddenly, all my big plans for myself didn't seem so important anymore. I soon found that the greatest joy in my life was the joy I saw in theirs.

"

Barack Obama

Author J.R.R. Tolkien was a dedicated dad to his three sons and one daughter. In order to not miss out on spending time with his children, Tolkien wrote his stories before sun rise each day. Several stories from his masterpieces – *The Hobbit* and *The Lord of the Rings* – began as improvised bedtime stories told to his children the night before.

A father is
someone you look
up to no matter how
tall you grow.

Parenting Paradox #3

Fatherhood is a beautiful dream in which you are unable to sleep.

"

It is easier to build strong children than to repair broken men.

"

Frederick Douglas

On average, a dad will spend 54 minutes per day trying to get their baby to sleep, adding up to almost

14 days

in their first year.

Source: *Independent*

You Know You're a Dad #4 When...

You take up DIY
as a hobby.

66

If you bungle raising your children, I don't think whatever else you do matters very much.

99

Jackie Kennedy

Dads are the coolest.
They always say
"yes" when Mum
said "no".

Fatherhood is like...
baking a cake.
A really messy,
ungrateful and
expensive cake.

66

I want to experience being a husband, experience being a father, experience, maybe, hopefully, someday being a grandfather, and all those things. When I die, I want to be exhausted.

99

Bryan Cranston

Dad Advice

When your kids hit the teenage years, get a dog. That way there will always be someone who's pleased to see you!

66

Now that I'm a
parent, I understand
why my father was
in a bad mood a lot.

99

Adam Sandler

Types of Dad #4:

The Driver

The Driver is a dad that *loves* to be in his car. He loves his car. He's happy to call shotgun the very second a child needs a ride anywhere – the further away the better. He loves to drive around the neighbourhood if only for the peace and quiet it brings outside of the house.

Are you the Driver?

66

To a father
growing old,
nothing is dearer
than a daughter.

99

Euripides

66

I cannot think
of any need in
childhood as strong
as the need for a
father's protection.

99

Sigmund Freud

66

Never is a man
more of a man
than when he is
the father of a
newborn.

99

Matthew McConaughey

Lies Dads Tell #3

If you go outside in cold
weather with wet hair,
you'll catch a cold.

Lies Dads Tell #4

Sitting too close to the
television will make you
go blind.

Dad Joke #9

How does a penguin build its house?

Igloos it together.

Shakespeare Does Dads #5

66

To you your father should be as a god, / One that composed your beauties, yea, and one / To whom you are but as a form in wax, / By him imprinted and within his power / To leave the figure or disfigure it.

99

A Midsummer Night's Dream, Act 1, Scene 1

"

Lately all my friends are worried they're turning into their fathers.
I'm worried I'm not.

"

Dan Zevin

Types of Dad #5:

The Napper

This type of dad is always falling asleep. It doesn't matter where: the sofa, the car, the in-laws, watching a movie, a child's birthday party. This dad loves to nap (especially on a Sunday afternoon) and could sleep through a herd of elephants playing in front of him. Often found in bed by 8pm. Are you the Napper?

CHAPTER
FOUR

Definitely
Awesome Dude

There are many types of dads in the world. They really do come in all shapes, sizes and smells. If you can, tell your dad you love them today - it'll make his day.

Fatherhood is like...
babysitting
24 hours a day.
And, at the end of
the day, you pay
the baby.

You Know You're a Dad #5 When...

You curse at an instruction manual and blame it for "being wrong".

Dad Joke #10

Why did the scarecrow win an award?

Because he was outstanding in his field.

In 2020, people in the USA spent more than

$17 billion*

(almost £12.8 billion) for Father's Day, with approximately 75 per cent of the 328 million citizens celebrating the national holiday.

Source: National Retail Federation / Statista

*$26.7 billion (£20.2 billion) was spent on mums, though.

According to one source, 71 per cent of dads use social media to keep the rest of the family up-to-date on what's going on with their kids.

Source: The Shelf

66

Never underestimate
kids' tenacity. Raising
a child is like wrestling
a small but relentless
opponent.

99

Stephen Colbert

Types of Dad #6:
The Techie

Gadgets, gizmos and gear
- anything that requires a
motherboard, batteries or remote
control - the Techie type of
dad is your man. The Techie
loves to fiddle and fondle with
computers, circuits and codes,
often breaking things that didn't
need fixing in the first place.
Are you the Techie?

66

Sometimes I'm amazed that my wife and I created two human beings from scratch yet struggle to assemble the most basic of IKEA cabinets.

99

John Kinnear

"

In my career, there's many things I've won and many things I've achieved, but for me, my greatest achievement is my children and my family.

"

David Beckham

Dad Joke #11

What's brown and sticky?

A stick.

Shakespeare Does Dads #6

"

It is a wise father
that knows his
own child.

"

Merchant Of Venice, Act 2, Scene 2

Dad-isms #4

1. It'll all end in tears!

2. I'm going to count to three.

3. I said no.

4. I'm not going to repeat myself.

5. You will always be my baby.

6. Do I look that stupid?

7. Because I said so.

8. Go play somewhere else!

9. Bored? How can you be bored? There's a whole world outside.

10. I've heard that lie before.

"

That is the thankless position of the father in the family – the provider for all, and the enemy of all.

"

J. August Strindberg

In the UK, in 2020, seven million Father's Day cards were sent.

For Mother's Day, 13 million cards were sent.

Source: Paper Mill Direct

Dad Joke #12

What do you call an elephant that doesn't matter?

An irrelephant.

You Know You're a Dad #6 When...

Your Amazon basket is full of fun things you would have bought if you weren't a dad.

Z Z Z Z Z Z Z

"

Remember: what dad really wants is a nap. Really.

"

Dave Barry

Types of Dad #7:
The Hiker

Anything to do with the Great
Outdoors, and you can guarantee
the Hiker is first at the door, wearing
his expensive boots. The Hiker is
a member of the National Trust
or Sierra Club, loves to use his legs
outside as often as possible and
encourages the family to follow him on
his wild dad-venturing – particularly
when it's wet, cold and dark.
Are you the Hiker?

66

When you're young,
you think your dad is
Superman. Then you
grow up, and you realize
he's just a regular guy
who wears a cape.

99

Dave Attell

Dad Joke #13

Is this pool safe for diving?

It deep ends.

"

One of the greatest things
a father can do for his
children is to love
their mother.

"

Howard W. Hunter

You Know You're a Dad #7 When...

You book a weekend break, desperate to have time away from your children.

(And then wish they were there).

66

The best way of training the young is to train yourself at the same time. Not to admonish them, but to be seen never doing that of which you would admonish them.

99

Plato

66

I think that my strong
determination for justice comes
from the very strong, dynamic
personality of my father...
I have rarely ever met a person
more fearless and courageous...
If I had a problem I could
always call Daddy.

99

Martin Luther King Jr

66

A two year old is kind of
like having a blender, but you
don't have a top for it.

99

Jerry Seinfeld

Dad Joke #14

What's ET short for?

Because he's only got tiny legs!

"

Just taught my
kids about taxes by
eating 38 per cent of
their ice cream.

"

Conan O'Brien

Types of Dad #8:
The DIY Dad

The DIY dad – such a rare sight
these days. These types of dads
can often be spotted shouting at
an instruction manual or kicking
a piece of IKEA furniture.
The DIY Dad is always proud of his
self-taught skills, no matter how
many YouTube videos he watched
in order to put up a simple shelf.
Are you the DIY Dad?

Shakespeare Does Dads #7

Who would be a father!

99

Othello, Act 1, Scene 1

Record-breaking Dad

Parents would move mountains for
their children. Dendi Sherpa, and his
16-year-old daughter, Ngim Chhamji
Sherpa, did the next best thing: they
climbed one. At the same time.
They are the first (and only) father
and daughter combo to reach the
peak of Mount Everest together.
The Nepalese duo reached
the summit on May 19, 2012.

*Sir Edmund Hillary created history on May 29, 1953,
becoming the first person to ascend the summit of
Mount Everest for the first time. His son, Peter, also reached
the peak in 1990.*

Fatherhood gets easier... until the next day when everything changes again.

Daddy Influencers to Follow*

1. @thedailydad
2. @howtobeadad
3. @oldschooldads
4. @daddownload
5. @dadandburied
6. @dadsayjokes
7. @theconscious_dad
8. @unlikelydad
9. @adayinthelifedad
10. @the_dadventurer
11. @dadofdivas
12. @this_father_life

*(*42 per cent of dads on social media follow
other dad influencers.)*

85 per cent

of U.S. fathers consider
being a dad the
best job in the world.

Source: U.S. Census Bureau

"

If you have never been hated by your child, you have never been a parent.

"

Bette Davis

> My father taught me to work, but not to love it. I never did like to work, and I don't deny it. I'd rather read, tell stories, crack jokes, talk, laugh - anything but work.

Abraham Lincoln